For Tommie Hill Sr.

To a love for a lifetime.

Love Barbara

Parker, Granny Needs A Kidney

Barbara A. Hill, EdD

"Hey Parker, give Granny a hug before I leave to go to dialysis."

"Diaaaaleeses?"

"What is that Granny?"

"Dia-lysis helps me live, when my kidneys
don't work."

"Granny what is a kidney, and what does it do?"

"I am so glad you asked."

"Lets explore that question."

"Granny what is a kidney, and what does it do?"

"I am so glad you asked."

"Lets explore that question."

Explore

Kidneys are bean shaped organs.

Humans have two Kidneys

They are located below the rib cage, one on each side of the spine.

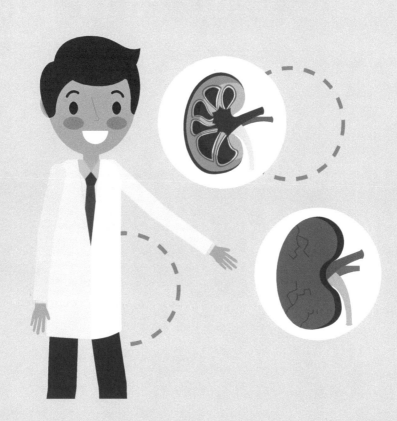

Kidneys Top 5 Jobs!

1. Filters Blood Through The Body
2. Help Control Blood Pressure Levels
3. Maintains Good Fluid Balance In The Body
4. Keeps Bones Healthy (Vitamin D, Calcium & Phosphorus)
5. Balance PH Levels.

Kidneys Do
So Much More!

Your Kidneys Need Pressure

Blood pressure is the force of blood pushing against the walls of your blood vessels as your heart pumps blood around your body.

Hypertension (high blood pressure) is a leading cause of kidney disease. It creeps up on you!

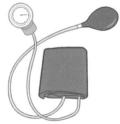

DID YOU KNOW...
Kidneys Help Make
RED BLOOD CELLS?

Red blood cells and
oxygen need to be made through
a hormone called...

ERYTHROPOIETIN

Erythropoietin

Kidneys Keep Bones Healthy

What do we do to keep our bones healthy?

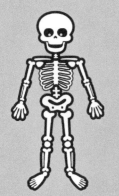

- Maintain proper levels of Vitamin D,
- Calcium
- and Phosphorus.

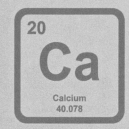

20
Ca
Calcium
40.078

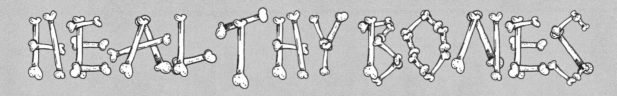

PH is needed for Acid Base Balance

The PH balance checks the balance of minerals in your blood
(like sodium, phosphorus and potassium).

"So you see Parker kidneys
have a big job."
"Okay, Granny but I still don't
know why you need dialysis."

"Parker Granny needs a kidney."
"My kidneys are not working
the way they should. My kidneys failed."
"Granny can we explore that more."
"Yes of course Parker."

Why do Kidneys Fail?

Did you know the leading cause of kidney failure in the United States is Diabetes?

The right diet can help prevent kidney failure.

THESE FOODS ARE GOOD FOR HEALTHY KIDNEYS.
BUT SOME OF THESE FOODS CAN BE HARMFUL TO SOMEONE LIVING WITH KIDNEY DISEASE

THESE FOODS CAN BE HARMFUL TO PEOPLE LIVING WITH KIDNEY DISEASE

PEOPLE WITH CKD HAVE TO WATCH THEIR PROTINE INTAKE. THE BODY MAY HAVE TROUBLE GETTING RID OF ALL THE WASTE PRODUCTS OF PROTEIN METABOLISM

AVOCADOS & TOMATOES ARE HIGH IN POTASSIUM. WITH KIDNEY FAILURE, THEY CAN BE HARMFUL.

AVOID DARK SODAS, CHIPS, CANNED FOOD AND SALT

BANANAS & POTATOES ARE HIGH IN POTASSIUM

The right diet for healthy kidneys may help prevent kidney disease

What is Dialysis?

Dialysis removes excess fluid, and cleans the blood, when the kidneys are not functioning to do these jobs.

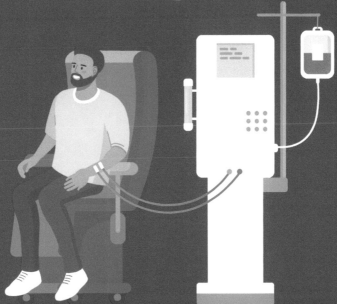

"Dialysis filters my blood through a
machine that cleans and removes excess fluid."
"Until I get a new kidney,
I have to have dialysis treatment 3x per week."
"Parker, do you have any more questions
about kidneys or dialysis?"

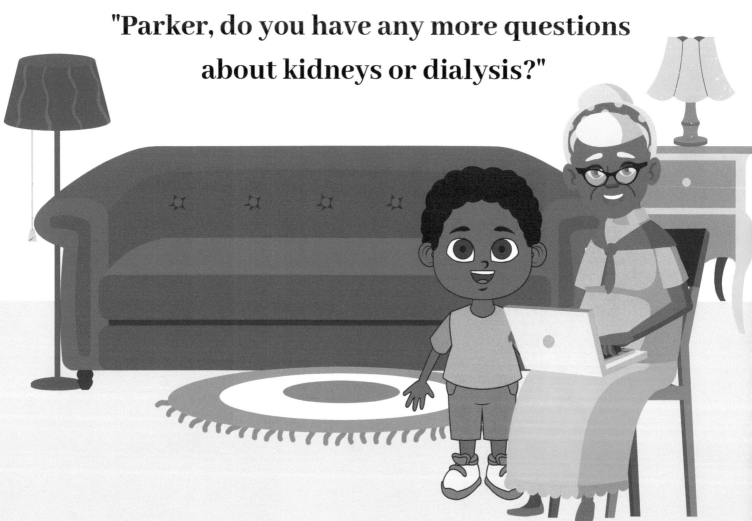

"Granny does dialysis hurt?"
"Sometimes you can experience
pain or discomfort, but the dialysis treatment
outweighs the bad."

Questions Page

What Questions Do You Have?

....

....

....

....

....

"Granny I hope and pray you get a kidney."

"Thank you me too honey."

"Where can we get one? Can we buy one?"

"I wish it worked that way dear."
"Another human being would have to give me one,
but it has to be a match for me to use their kidney."

"Well we better get moving to find you one Granny!"

"Parker you are correct,
those are our next steps."
"We are going to find Granny a kidney!"

Lesson Check!
What Have
You Learned?

Notes Page

....

....

....

Draw a Kidney in the Box

"Granny I packed you a lunch for dialysis,
so that your pressure won't get low."
"Thank you my grandson, you have learned so
much about kidneys and dialysis I am so proud of you."

Printed in the USA
CPSIA information can be obtained
at www.ICGtesting.com
LVHW071959150924
790968LV00002B/58

9798869197610